General observations on executory devises, or on the power of individuals to prescribe, by testamentary dispositions, the particular future uses to be made of their property. With the last will of Peter Thellusson The second edition.

Jean Louis De Lolme

General observations on executory devises, or on the power of individuals to prescribe, by testamentary dispositions, the particular future uses to be made of their property. Occasioned by the last will of ... Peter Thellusson, ... By John Lewis de Lolme, The second edition.

De Lolme, Jean Louis
ESTCID: T098199
Reproduction from British Library
In fact, a supplement to the first edition, p.37 (sig.L1) intended to replace p.37 in the first edition.
London : printed by W. and C. Spilsbury. Published by J. Richardson and Son; C. Law; T. Egerton; and W. Clarke, 1800.
[2],37-49,[1]p. ; 4°

Eighteenth Century
Collections Online
Print Editions

Gale ECCO Print Editions

Relive history with *Eighteenth Century Collections Online*, now available in print for the independent historian and collector. This series includes the most significant English-language and foreign-language works printed in Great Britain during the eighteenth century, and is organized in seven different subject areas including literature and language; medicine, science, and technology; and religion and philosophy. The collection also includes thousands of important works from the Americas.

The eighteenth century has been called "The Age of Enlightenment." It was a period of rapid advance in print culture and publishing, in world exploration, and in the rapid growth of science and technology – all of which had a profound impact on the political and cultural landscape. At the end of the century the American Revolution, French Revolution and Industrial Revolution, perhaps three of the most significant events in modern history, set in motion developments that eventually dominated world political, economic, and social life.

In a groundbreaking effort, Gale initiated a revolution of its own: digitization of epic proportions to preserve these invaluable works in the largest online archive of its kind. Contributions from major world libraries constitute over 175,000 original printed works. Scanned images of the actual pages, rather than transcriptions, recreate the works *as they first appeared.*

Now for the first time, these high-quality digital scans of original works are available via print-on-demand, making them readily accessible to libraries, students, independent scholars, and readers of all ages.

For our initial release we have created seven robust collections to form one the world's most comprehensive catalogs of 18th century works.

Initial Gale ECCO Print Editions collections include:

History and Geography

Rich in titles on English life and social history, this collection spans the world as it was known to eighteenth-century historians and explorers. Titles include a wealth of travel accounts and diaries, histories of nations from throughout the world, and maps and charts of a world that was still being discovered. Students of the War of American Independence will find fascinating accounts from the British side of conflict.

Social Science

Delve into what it was like to live during the eighteenth century by reading the first-hand accounts of everyday people, including city dwellers and farmers, businessmen and bankers, artisans and merchants, artists and their patrons, politicians and their constituents. Original texts make the American, French, and Industrial revolutions vividly contemporary.

Medicine, Science and Technology

Medical theory and practice of the 1700s developed rapidly, as is evidenced by the extensive collection, which includes descriptions of diseases, their conditions, and treatments. Books on science and technology, agriculture, military technology, natural philosophy, even cookbooks, are all contained here.

Literature and Language

Western literary study flows out of eighteenth-century works by Alexander Pope, Daniel Defoe, Henry Fielding, Frances Burney, Denis Diderot, Johann Gottfried Herder, Johann Wolfgang von Goethe, and others. Experience the birth of the modern novel, or compare the development of language using dictionaries and grammar discourses.

Religion and Philosophy

The Age of Enlightenment profoundly enriched religious and philosophical understanding and continues to influence present-day thinking. Works collected here include masterpieces by David Hume, Immanuel Kant, and Jean-Jacques Rousseau, as well as religious sermons and moral debates on the issues of the day, such as the slave trade. The Age of Reason saw conflict between Protestantism and Catholicism transformed into one between faith and logic -- a debate that continues in the twenty-first century.

Law and Reference

This collection reveals the history of English common law and Empire law in a vastly changing world of British expansion. Dominating the legal field is the *Commentaries of the Law of England* by Sir William Blackstone, which first appeared in 1765. Reference works such as almanacs and catalogues continue to educate us by revealing the day-to-day workings of society.

Fine Arts

The eighteenth-century fascination with Greek and Roman antiquity followed the systematic excavation of the ruins at Pompeii and Herculaneum in southern Italy; and after 1750 a neoclassical style dominated all artistic fields. The titles here trace developments in mostly English-language works on painting, sculpture, architecture, music, theater, and other disciplines. Instructional works on musical instruments, catalogs of art objects, comic operas, and more are also included.

The BiblioLife Network

This project was made possible in part by the BiblioLife Network (BLN), a project aimed at addressing some of the huge challenges facing book preservationists around the world. The BLN includes libraries, library networks, archives, subject matter experts, online communities and library service providers. We believe every book ever published should be available as a high-quality print reproduction; printed on-demand anywhere in the world. This insures the ongoing accessibility of the content and helps generate sustainable revenue for the libraries and organizations that work to preserve these important materials.

The following book is in the "public domain" and represents an authentic reproduction of the text as printed by the original publisher. While we have attempted to accurately maintain the integrity of the original work, there are sometimes problems with the original work or the micro-film from which the books were digitized. This can result in minor errors in reproduction. Possible imperfections include missing and blurred pages, poor pictures, markings and other reproduction issues beyond our control. Because this work is culturally important, we have made it available as part of our commitment to protecting, preserving, and promoting the world's literature.

GUIDE TO FOLD-OUTS MAPS and OVERSIZED IMAGES

The book you are reading was digitized from microfilm captured over the past thirty to forty years. Years after the creation of the original microfilm, the book was converted to digital files and made available in an online database.

In an online database, page images do not need to conform to the size restrictions found in a printed book. When converting these images back into a printed bound book, the page sizes are standardized in ways that maintain the detail of the original. For large images, such as fold-out maps, the original page image is split into two or more pages

Guidelines used to determine how to split the page image follows:

• Some images are split vertically; large images require vertical and horizontal splits.
• For horizontal splits, the content is split left to right.
• For vertical splits, the content is split from top to bottom.
• For both vertical and horizontal splits, the image is processed from top left to bottom right.

GENERAL OBSERVATIONS

ON

EXECUTORY DEVISES,

OR

ON THE POWER OF INDIVIDUALS

TO PRESCRIBE, BY TESTAMENTARY DISPOSITIONS,

THE PARTICULAR FUTURE USES TO BE MADE OF THEIR PROPERTY.

Occasioned by the last Will *of the late* Mr. Peter Thellusson, *of London.*

BY

JOHN LEWIS DE LOLME, LL. D.

AUTHOR OF THE BOOK ON THE "*CONSTITUTION OF ENGLAND.*"

THE SECOND EDITION.

LONDON

Printed by *W* and *C. Spilsbury, No* 57, *Snowhill, London*

PUBLISHED BY J RICHARDSON AND SON, UNDER THE ROYAL-EXCHANGE, C. LAW, AVE MARIA-LANE, T. EGERTON, WHITEHALL, AND W CLARKE, NEW BOND STREET

1800.

REFERENCES in the following Pages.

At the end of the fecond Paragraph, add, *See back, page* 10.
In page 24, laft line but two, inftead of *page* 19, read 19 *and* 10.
In page 34, laft line, inftead of *pages* 18, 19 read 18, 10.
In page 35, feventh line, inftead of *pages* 18, 19, read 18, 10.

Executors who engage to carry on ſuch *Truſts* do, in fact, reſolutely engage to enter upon, and to go through, ſuch courſes of
proceeding.

They are bold Men: they ceitainly are no Cowards. The chriſ-
tian name of one of the three *Executors* named in the *Will* of the
late Mr. Peter Thelluſſon, is *Emperor*—(*Emperor* John Woodſoid).
Moſt likely the conſideration of their having an Emperor among
them, has given them hope of being able to carry on their *Truſt*.

Their courage is evident. They are to deal in landed Pioperty,
Manors, Freeholds, and moſt widely-extended purchaſes: it is all
to be open buſineſs.

POSTSCRIPT.

A DESCRIPTION has been given, in the preceding pages, of
the ſtate of hoſtility and breach of the peace againſt Mankind in
which the Executor of an *Executory Deviſe* continues moving. He
is in ſuch a ſtate of breach of the peace by his aſſumption of authority over Mankind, and by being, in fact, inveſted with a power
of reſolutely repulſing and diſmiſſing the claims, complaints and
objections of all ſuch Individuals as he happens to have dealings
with, relatively to the *deviſed* Pioperty. Theſe reſolute diſmiſſals
of the claims, complaints and objections of Individuals, an *Executor* performs by means of reſolute allegations of the ſupeiior duty
he owes to the *deviſed* Property, and to his Employer the *Teſtatoi*,
whoſe approbation he nevei can poſſibly obtain foi the diſcharging
of any claim, or attending to any complaint or objection.

Abundant inſtances of ſuch *reſolute diſmiſſals* have been given in
the preceding pages; and the obſervation has alſo been made, that
the *Executor*'s alledged ſuperior duty to his Teſtator, and his reſo-

L   lute

lute *difmiffing power* arifing from fuch alledged fuperior duty, are moreover ftrengthened and *affirmed* in Courts of Law by means of their affirmation or adoption of the devifing *Will*.

In thofe preceding pages I went no farther than defcribing the above-mentioned ftate of hoftility and courfe of breach of the peace againft Mankind. I forbore pointing out and fully afcertaining the high and truly ferious degree of illegality with which the practice of *Executory Devifes* is farther connected; becaufe I was afraid of bringing into a danger of immediate *forfeiture*, not only the Property of the late Mr. Thelluffon, but alfo that whole mafs of *devifed* Property which lies in the Court of Chancery, tied down to ceitain fixed *Ufes*, by the continued *Wills* and commands of *Mafters* who never can be confulted with; and tied down, too, in fome cafes, for half, and even whole centuries.

But the danger of *forfeiture* in regard to the above-mentioned Properties is now over. Since the firft publication of the preceding part of this Pamphlet, a Committee of Judges have made the fame miftake as had been made by other Judges before them. That Committee have not only paufed nearly five months on the matter, thereby fhewing they were perplexed, but have even at laft *affirmed* the late Mr. Thelluffon's *Will*; by which they have made it manifeft that they continued to miftake, or mifs feeing, the truly ferious illegality which is connected with the practice of *Executory Devifes*. Since Judges, acting with the moft perfect freedom from any malevolent intentions againft the Laws of the Country, have miftaken the real ftate of the cafe, it follows that common Teftators muft be allowed to have merely fallen into *miftakes*, and to have been free from guilt, when devifing and ftrictly tying down their Properties to *unmodifiable Ufes*, to be executed by *Executors* whom no Courts of Law or any living Perfons could remove: the confequence of which obfervation is, that the Properties devifed by thofe Teftatois in the manner here defcribed, have become faved from *forfeiture*. By their *affirmation* of the late Mr. Thelluffon's *Will*, the Committee of Judges have, in fact, covered all the above-mentioned Properties with the mantle of their own guiltlefs, unfpotted intentions.

I am

I am now proceeding to shew the high degree of illegality which really attends the practice of *Executory Devises*. This high illegality directly appears from the very allegations which are made with an intent to excuse that practice. The Gentlemen of the Law excuse an *Executor* engaged in the practice here mentioned, no better than by positively making professions of this Executor moreover committing other acts of most serious guilt, which professions are no doubt unthinkingly made, and without any bad intention.

For instance, they excuse an *Executor* in regard to the engagement he has taken to disobey all such Acts of Parliament as happen to be passed contrary to his Trust, (*see back, from page* 4 *to* 10) by alledging that the Executor, in such case, *forbears* to execute his Trust. Very well; but what does the Executor do with the *devised* Property, after he finds he *cannot* execute the *Trust*? does he return or deliver back the Land, when he finds he cannot cut the Timber?* does he return the Property of any kind to the *Proprietor?* No; he keeps it. Therefore he keeps it as stolen Property, or embezzled Property.

If, after the Master of a Ship has taken in corn for exportation to France or America, an Act prohibiting such exportation happens to be passed, this Master of the Ship is not to keep the corn, sending it to his own warehouses on shore, by way of solacing himself under the grief he feels on account of the passing of the Act: he must apply to the Owner of the corn, and tell him, " Sir, take your corn back, and discharge your duty yourself to the Act of Parliament." If a Porter is sent to carry a deposit of money to a Banker's counting-house, and he finds the counting-house shut, either because the Clerks have thought proper to go home, or the Bankers have given up business, the Porter is not to march off with the

---

* This is an allusion to what is observed in page 9, relatively to the prescription which is laid by Mr. Thellusson's *Will* upon the Executor to cut the Timber upon the *devised* Land. Now, an Act of Parliament for prohibiting or very much restricting the cutting of Timber may be soon expected to take place, because that Commission which was appointed a few years ago for inquiring into the state of Timber over the whole Country, have concluded their Report with an earnest recommendation that extensive restrictions may be laid on the cutting of Timber.

the money as his perquifite: he muft carry this money back to the Perfon who fent him with it; telling him, " Sir, take your money back; I cannot deliver it; try, if you choofe, to deliver it yourfelf." If a Man fends a Groom to take a Horfe to certain livery-ftables which he names to him, and the Groom finds the ftables fhut, he is not to ride away with the Horfe: he muft feek the Owner, and reftore the Horfe to him. To attempt therefore to excufe an Executor, by alledging that he complies with Acts of Parliament by difobeying the *Truft,* but that he neverthelefs continues after that to keep the trufted or *devifed* Property, is excufing him by profeffing that this Executor puts himfelf in a very ferious ftate of guilt, in a fituation of real theft and embezzlement.

I may, befides, obferve that an *Executor,* in fuch a cafe, violates his Oath; fince he has moreover taken an Oath to obferve the *Truft.* however I fhall not go farther into that fubject, becaufe the violation of an Oath relates to divine more than to human Laws. Continuing therefore to fpeak only of human Laws, I fhall farther mention that an Executor, by the mere taking of an Oath to the Teftator his Employer, does in fact offend againft the Statutes of *Præmunire.* Thofe Statutes prohibit the taking of Oaths to any Being whatever, other than the governing Power of the Country. The mere *tendering* of fuch Oaths, or requefting that fuch Oaths may be taken, is highly illegal. There is therefore a ferious degree of illegality in an Executor *actually* taking an Oath to his Teftator or private Employer; from whofe Property, it muft be farther obferved, he cannot be removed.

The Gentlemen of the Law alfo attempt to excufe an Executor in regard to that power which he affumes, of refolutely difmiffing the claims of Individuals, which he does, as before mentioned, by alledging his fuperior duty to an Employer whofe approbation he never can obtain for the difcharge of any claim: a duty which he has moreover caufed to be ftrengthened and *affirmed* by Courts of Law. Thefe Gentlemen fay, if an Executor exerts his *difmiffing* power with too much obftinacy, he may be fued before a Court of Law, and be be compelled by Judgments to difcharge claims. Very well; but he is fo compelled by a violation of *Magna Charta.* For, how is he fued? he is fued in his own, the Executor's name. And how is Judgment given againft him? alfo in his own name. And with what Property is he made to pay? is he made to pay with his own Property, the Property of him, the Executor, againft whom Judgment has been given? No; he is made to pay out of the *devifed* Property, out of the Property of his Teftator, againft whom no Judgment has been given. Now, this kind of Law-proceeding, by which the Property of a Proprietor is come upon againft whom *no Judgment* has been given, is contrary to the 29th Article of *Magna Charta,* in which the King declared in behalf of the Subject, " Neither fhall we go upon him, nor fhall we fend " upon him, unlefs it be by the Judgment of his Peers, or by " Acts or Statutes of Parliament."

I fhall add a fact which the Reader will think fomewhat remarkable. When an Executor happens to defert his *Truft,* either becaufe he is become carelefs, or perhaps does not find from it the advantage he had expected for himfelf, the Courts of Law punifh him by allowing all demands and fuits to continue to go againft him in the fame manner as before, though he has caft off the Teftator's Property, and they then make him really pay out of his own Property, that is his punifhment: fo that he is punifhed by being *compelled* to obferve *Magna Charta.* Not fo when he continues to follow his *Truft* to the fatisfaction of the Courts: he is then re-warded, and his reward is by being indulged with a *permiffion* to violate *Magna Charta.*

The Gentlemen of the Law alfo *excufe* the *Executor* of the *unmodi-fiable* prefcriptions of his Teftator, by alledging that this *Executor,* if he be a little tender-hearted, or if cautious forbearance becomes requifite, may not perhaps quite invariably exert his power of refo-lutely difmiffing the claims proffered by Individuals. he may fome-times difcharge fuch claims of his own accord, and without waiting till, by judgment being given againft *himfelf,* he is compelled, in the King's name, to pay out of the Property of his Teftator, againft whom no judgment has been given, and thus to violate *Magna Charta.* Very true; but then the Executor, when thus *willingly*

M   paying,

paying, pays with serious guilt of another kind; he pays by a real embezzlement; since he pays without the possible knowledge and approbation of his Employer. What honest Man, what Man of honour would accept a payment from a Servant or Clerk who should say, " Sir, I will pay you out of my Master's Property, though he shall never have knowledge of such payment ?"

In short, it turns out, that the Gentlemen of the Law *excuse* an Executor by professing that, to such Claimants or *Demandants* as prove rather too sturdy for him, the Executor says, " Sir, I will pay you, if, by suing me in that manner in which an Executor is to be proceeded against, you choose to violate *Magna Charta* along with me: let us violate *Magna Charta* together; and you shall have your money or claim." To other Claimants the Executor says, " Sir, I will pay you of my own accord; but I must embezzle the money first; and yourself do join with me; do consent and accede to the embezzlement by accepting the payment of the money, though I am telling you that the Testator, my Master, shall never, at any time, have knowledge of such payment."

Many honest Claimants rather choose to lose their dues than accede to such doings; and their losses constitute a part of an Executor's profits. One honest Claimant of that sort I may name, who is a very important one, both in regard to *respectability*, and to the nature of the claims; and that is Government itself. Taxes are constantly forborne being levied, when the Property out of which the Tax is to be paid, appears directly, and on the very first inspection of the Case, to be *devised* or *trusted* Property. Government will not consent to a Tax being levied on the Property of a Proprietor who has not had, nor can possibly have had, *any notice* of the Tax. When the Chancellor of the Exchequer laid his Proposal of the *Assessed* Taxes before Parliament, he expressed a deal of honest anxiety on the subject of devised Property; and at last he concluded on the honest side of the question, by allowing such devised Property to enjoy an exemption. And I have been told that the present Tax upon *Income* is likewise forborne being levied upon *devised* Property.

Nor does Government lose its dues merely in regard to that friendly assistance and those retributions it has a right to expect, on account of the protection it is continually affording to *devised* Property (sometimes amounting to prodigious stocks or masses), as well as to every other kind of Property; but Government also loses its claims in cases of *Forfeitures.* The Gentlemen of the Law have positively obtained to have the point established, that no act of an Executor can produce the forfeiture of the *devised* Property. An Executor may use the ships and stores of his *Testator,* for the purpose of sending supplies to an Enemy; and they cannot be touched: they are the Property of a Master against whom no Judgment can be given. (Those Ships cannot be touched otherwise than in the manner of a common seizure made at Sea, by being caught in the very act, and in the very time.)

An Executor may allow the use of the lands and fields of his *Testator* for the purpose of treasonable meetings, and even rebellious encampments, and Government cannot seize upon those fields: no Judgment can be given against the *Testator,* who is the Master. An Executor may use the Horses and Chaises of his *Testator* for the purpose of carrying on a treasonable correspondence across the Country, and they are not liable to any forfeiture. The Testator is the Master of them: he is a Master against whom no Judgment can be given: he *can do no wrong*; his Property *can do no wrong:* he stops the hand of Government itself.

Since Government has thus given way, it is easy to understand how an *Executor* may succeed in engrossing masses of Property at the expence of private, scattered Individuals, easily overawed by this Executor's power of resolutely dismissing claims, complaints and objections of any kind, by means of a bold allegation of the superior duty he owes to the Testator, his Employer, whose approbation he cannot possibly obtain for the discharging of any claim, or attending to any objection; which alledged duty has been strengthened and *affirmed* by Courts of Law.

A very important observation must be introduced in this place, which is, that the mere circumstance of a Testator, against whom *no Judgment can be given,* being allowed to continue to be a *Proprietor,* is, of itself and without any farther consideration, a most serious illegality, it is an infringement on the Statutes of *Praemunire.* And any Man who pretends to be an Executor or Servant to such a *Proprietor,* joins in such an infringement, and takes upon himself the guilt of the *posthumous* continuation of the same.

It

It may perhaps be said, that the Case of the Administration of a *Minor*'s Property is similar to the Case of an *Executorship:* is not an *Executor* like a *Guardian?* No such thing: an Executor is not like a Guardian. A Guardian has always his *Minor* and legal *Proprietor* along with him, by whose presence he constantly gives legality to his proceedings; and that is the reason for which the Guardian to the Property is always Guardian to the Person. Suits at Law are not carried on in the Guardian's name: all Suits, either *pro* or *con,* are in the *Minor*'s name; who is even frequently made to appear, and whom it is always in the power of the Guardian to produce. Likewise, when a Guardian *willingly* pays or discharges claims, he does so in a manner in the company of his Minor, to whom he is a Guide and Assistant.

In short, a Guardian and his Minor, together, form a *legal Man,* a *legal Proprietor,* who is free from offence against the Statutes of *Præmunire;* who may be legally sued and compelled to pay without any violation of *Magna Charta;* and by whom claims may also be willingly discharged with legality, without embezzlement, and without trepanning any Individual who receives a payment into an accession to such embezzlement, that is, into a consent to receive such payment notwithstanding it be admitted that the Proprietor, out of whose Property the payment is made, is never, at any time, to have knowledge of the same, as is always expressly admitted when an *Executor* pays.

To which add, that a Guardian is positively liable to being removed; even upon his Minor's Petition; but an Executor cannot be removed;—he cannot be removed from the management of the Property of the Testator, his Master, without the consent of that Master.

It is not to be denied, however, that Administrations of Minor's Properties by Guardians are frequently taken advantage of, for carrying on engrossing schemes at the expence of other classes of Individuals. But the abuses can never reach such lengths as those do which arise from *Executorships:* and, in fact, when an engrossing scheme is particularly aimed at, under cover of a *Minority,* the expedient of additionally employing an Executor is always resorted to by a Testator. The time of the duration of an Executorship may,

besides,

beſides, be made to be incomparably longer than the time of the duration of a Minority. *(See back, pages 2, and 20, 21.)*

The Practice of *Executory Deviſes* is moreover highly contrary to the intent of the Statutes of Mortmain : I mean thoſe Statutes by which Property, eſpecially in land, is reſtricted in a conſiderable degree from being deviſed by laſt *Wills,* or otherwiſe transferred, to *Corporate Bodies.* It ſeems to me that Lawyers, either in this or other Countries, have not pointed out the trueſt reaſons for which Statutes of this ſort have been paſſed or decreed by all Governments. One of the true reaſons ſeems to be, the power which ſuch *Cor-porate Bodies* derive from their weight, and the number of their Aſſociates, for the purpoſe of ſetting at defiance or turning aſide the claims, complaints and objections of other Individuals ; thereby aſſuming an advantage againſt the reſt of Mankind which is not enjoyed againſt them. And the means by which theſe *Corporate Bodies* aſſume ſuch overruling power over the claims, complaints and objections of other Individuals, is, in fact, by *hiding* themſelves, that is to ſay, by making it difficult for other Individuals to find out and aſcertain a real *Proprietor* among the Aſſociates who compoſe ſuch Corporate Bodies. Every one of theſe Aſſociates refers to the other Aſſociates, and ſays, "You muſt catch the time when the Corporation is ſitting : they may then attend to your allegation, and then perhaps deliberate upon it, and perhaps alſo come to ſome determination about it, by taking and aſcertaining a *Majority* among themſelves." And even then the buſineſs is not ſettled ; for it may become difficult for individual Strangers to prove and clearly point out ſuch *Majority* to other Men. The caſe is not by any means ſo in regard to *Partnerſhips* among Merchants. A Partner in a Trading Houſe is not to ſay, "We are five Partners ; you muſt catch us all " five together (if you can) ; and then we may perhaps pay you." If *Partnerſhips* had been inſtituted on ſuch a Plan, they would have been found to be unbearable, but they are not ſo. every Partner binds the whole Partnerſhip by his *ſingle* ſignature, and he alſo *ſingly* and legally pays for the whole Partnerſhip. Every Partner in Trade is made to be an *whole Proprietor,* not allowed to *hide himſelf* by any put-off and reference to other Partners

It muſt however be confeſſed, that, when a real viſible *Pro-prietor,* or a real viſible *Proprietorſhip,* has been once aſcertained

N   in in a Corporate Body relatively to any affair by individual Strangers, that affair is thenceforwards managed and terminated with legality, that is to fay, without trepanning fuch Strangers into violations of *Magna Charta,* or into acceffions to embezzlements, previoufly to allowing fuch Strangers their dues. But, in the cafe of an *Executory Devife,* the Proprietor or Teftator is not merely *hidden* for fome fhorter or longer time : it is admitted that he never can poffibly be found and produced. To which add, that, when thofe *illegal* advantages which are exprefsly and purpofely defigned to be taken of Mankind by the bold allegation of fuch *perpetual abfence,* appear too intolerable, and cautious forbearance becomes abfolutely requifite, the expedient is ufed, of flinching and fkulking from fuch advantages, as above obferved, by committing offences againft *Magna Charta,* as well as againft the laws directly relative to embezzlements, and, by profeffions of fuch fkulking offences being committed, the practice of Executory Devifes continues to be *excufed.* From which it follows that this practice is, all together, a worfe cafe, by far, than any of thofe which are exprefsly named in the Statutes of *Mortmain.*

It is enacted by the Statute of the 13th year of Queen ELIZA-BETH, that, if a Merchant hides himfelf for a very few days only, even in his own Houfe, and even alfo though his Clerks and Servants may continue faying, they expect him every hour, fuch Merchant is oufted from his Property; which is immediately taken poffeffion of for fuch Perfons as may prove their claims. How therefore can it be pretended that any Being, with the name of being a *Teftator,* or with any name, can continue to be a *Proprietor* during a period of perhaps an hundred years, or more, though it is admitted that he cannot be confulted with, in any fhape, by his Executors or Servants, or any Perfon, during the whole time ; and that, even after the expiration of that time, he is not to make any appearance ?*

Thofe

---

* The Reader may perhaps wifh to know what period of time is allowed for the *duration* of an *Executorfhip* The rule is this A Teftator may caufe his property to continue to be *unmodifably* managed by his Executor and Servant, that is to fay, may caufe the power over the property to continue in himfelf, the Teftator, during the lives of any fuch number of Perfons in being at the time of his deceafe, as he choofes to name. The Teftator, it is faid, may take up the *Red Book* or Court Calendar, and prefcribe that the *Executorfhip* is to laft during the lives of all the Perfons named in the book, as well as of any other Perfons or Children, either juft born, or in the womb, whom he may choofe to name befides And if

Thoſe Lawyers who undertake to write in a proper form ſuch laſt *Wills* as are intended to contain Executory Deviſes, always take care to introduce a clauſe by which the Teſtator *ratifies beforehand* all ſuch Deeds preſcribed to be performed by the Executors, as require formally-authenticated ratifications from Proprietors, for their being valid. I mention this by way of ſhewing how truly Lawyers conſider a *Teſtator* as continuing to be the *Proprietor* during the whole time the Executorſhip is to laſt, and to be the Maſter and Employer of the Executor; who, in fact, cannot be removed otherwiſe than with this Maſter's conſent. To which muſt be added, that this Teſtator is thus made to give his ratification and approbation to things and deeds, of the true performances of which he never can have any *knowledge*. If, in the performing of thoſe deeds afterwards, any fraud happens to be committed by the Executor againſt the Teſtator's Property, or againſt other Perſons, or by other Perſons againſt him, the Teſtator nevertheleſs ratifies it all.

A Gentleman of the Law who has lately written on the ſubject of *Executory Deviſes*, calls ſuch engroſſing ſchemes as have a tendency, by means of ſuch *Deviſes*, to engroſs ſcores of millions, and whole Counties, by no worſe a name than ſchemes of *poſthumous avarice*. But ſome farther definitions might be given of ſuch engroſſing *Executory Deviſes*; no matter whether they are intended for effecting prodigious engroſſments, or only middling ones.

The engroſſing ſcheme carried on by the Executor and Servant of the Teſtator, might rather be called a poſthumous ſtate of infringement upon the Statutes of *Præmunire*, by the power of Property being allowed to continue to be in a *Proprietor* againſt whom

110

at the time of the deceaſe of the laſt Liver of all thoſe Perſons, that other Perſon who is to take the property happens to be a Minor, even juſt born, the twenty-one years of the Minority are to be added to the duration of the *Executorſhip* preſcribed by the Teſtator, inſtead of a *Guardian* being appointed both to the perſon and to the property of ſuch Minor, which lengthening of the duration is intended as a kind of *douceur* in favour of the practice of *Executaſhip*.—It has been obſerved, in page 10, that an Executor may continue his Executorſhip by Aſſigns, named by him in his own laſt Will (See alſo the Note in page 12)

It may be aſked, what is the reaſon for which the duration of an Executorſhip, or continuation of an unavoidable engroſſing management of dev[i]ſed property, is thus confined to a century, or thereabouts, inſtead of being allowed to continue for a longer time, or even to be perpetual? I never was able to underſtand the reaſon that is given for ſuch limitation. It ſeemed to me that the reaſon is merely becauſe, though thoſe Perſons who had originally ſettled ſuch limitation, could ſwallow one pound of abſurd illegality, they could not ſwallow two pounds.

no Judgment can be given. The same engroffing scheme also is a posthumous state of breach of the peace against the bulk of Mankind, by being an affumption of authority over them, and a power of refolutely difmiffing their claims, complaints and objections of any kind, by means of the Executor's bold allegation of the fuperior duty he owes to his *Employer* the Teftator, with whom, he refolutely fays, he never can poffibly confult, and never can obtain his approbation for the difcharging of any claim, or attending to any objection; which alledged duty has been ftrengthened and *affirmed* by Courts of Law.

To which add, that, when the advantages which are intended to be derived from this posthumous complicate state of illegality, appear too intolerable, and cautious forbearance becomes requifite, the expedient is ufed, of flinching and fkulking from fuch advantages by means of fkulking commiffions of ftill greater illegalities; that is to fay, by fkulking offences against *Magna Charta*, and also against the Laws directly relative to embezzlement, and by trepanning other Individuals, when obftinate and unfubmiffive, into acceffions to fuch offences, for the fake of obtaining redrefs by fuch means.

And for what ufeful purpofe is that *posthumous* complicate state of offence against the Statutes of *Præmunire*, and against the peace of Mankind, as well as thofe fkulking commiffions of ftill greater illegalities by which fuch *posthumous* illegal state continues to be excufed? The whole is for the purpofe that posthumous avarice, or posthumous vanity, if the Reader prefers calling it fo, may be gratified; and that too, with fuch an extent of engroffment as other Individuals can never finally effect by any legal trade or other purfuit; that is to fay, other Individuals unaffifted by any law fiction and management, and left, with their own individual weaknefs, and own individual unaffifted flippancy, to encounter either the real oppofition, or the contempt, reproaches, and refentment of other Men.—And the effected engroffment may even perhaps confift of fcores of millions, of Manors, of Freeholds, and the political rights of whole Counties. *(See back, pages* 25, 26, 31).

It muft therefore be admitted, that certain Gentlemen of the Law fhew a deal of indulgence, when they beftow no worfe a name than the name of *avarice* on the engroffing fchemes above-mentioned. They likewife fhew their indulgence when they content

themfelves

themſelves with blaming the ſame engroſſing ſchemes, by merely obſerving that they have a tendency to accumulation. I ſhall, by the bye, obſerve, that there is no great harm yet in *accumulation* merely : deſigns of accumulation are, we ſee, the general aim of Trade and Buſineſs amongſt Men : there is, as juſt ſaid, no great harm in that ; but the great point to be ſtrictly attended to and ob-ſerved, is, that *accumulation* be performed *with legality*. Accumu-lation, *without legality*, is very bad, moſt certainly.

The ſame Gentlemen alſo manifeſt their very great indulgence and tenderneſs, when they go on merely obſerving and lamenting that engroſſing ſchemes purſued under cover of Executory Deviſes, have the effect of preventing Property from being *enjoyed*. But neither is there any great harm yet in forbearance from enjoyment, provided there is no forbearance *from legality* nothing is yet very much amiſs, if, while forbearance from enjoyment continues to be practiſed, care is taken that *duties* ſhould continue to be performed to other Men, and to Law, and to Legality.

In ſhort, mere accumulation, and mere forbearance from enjoy-ment, are tolerably harmleſs things : but they are bad, very bad indeed, when they are united with that ſtate of complicate, high, exceſſive illegality above deſcribed.

Since ſuch complicate high illegality attends the practice of *Executory Deviſes*, it follows that no expedient of ſhortening the time of its duration can be called an *amendment*, and that the practice cannot, in fact, be otherwiſe amended than by being ſet aſide.

The caſe is different in regard to adminiſtrations of the properties of Minors by *Guardians* to the Perſons. That degree of irregu-larity which exiſts in ſuch a mode of adminiſtering Property, may be conſiderably amended. *(See back, from page 19 to 21).* And ſuch ſhare of irregularity as may be thought fit to continued, may be indulged and excuſed, for the reaſons mentioned in the ſame pages, becauſe there is no ſerious illegality *neceſſarily* inherent in that mode of adminiſtering Property, by *mere* Guardians to the Perſons and the Properties together.

Printed by W. and C. Spilsbury, Snowhill, London.

CPSIA information can be obtained
at www.ICGtesting.com
Printed in the USA
BVHW060520070223
657977BV00012B/483